The Toy Soldier

Written by Karen L Chaney

Illustrated by Lee Chemlen

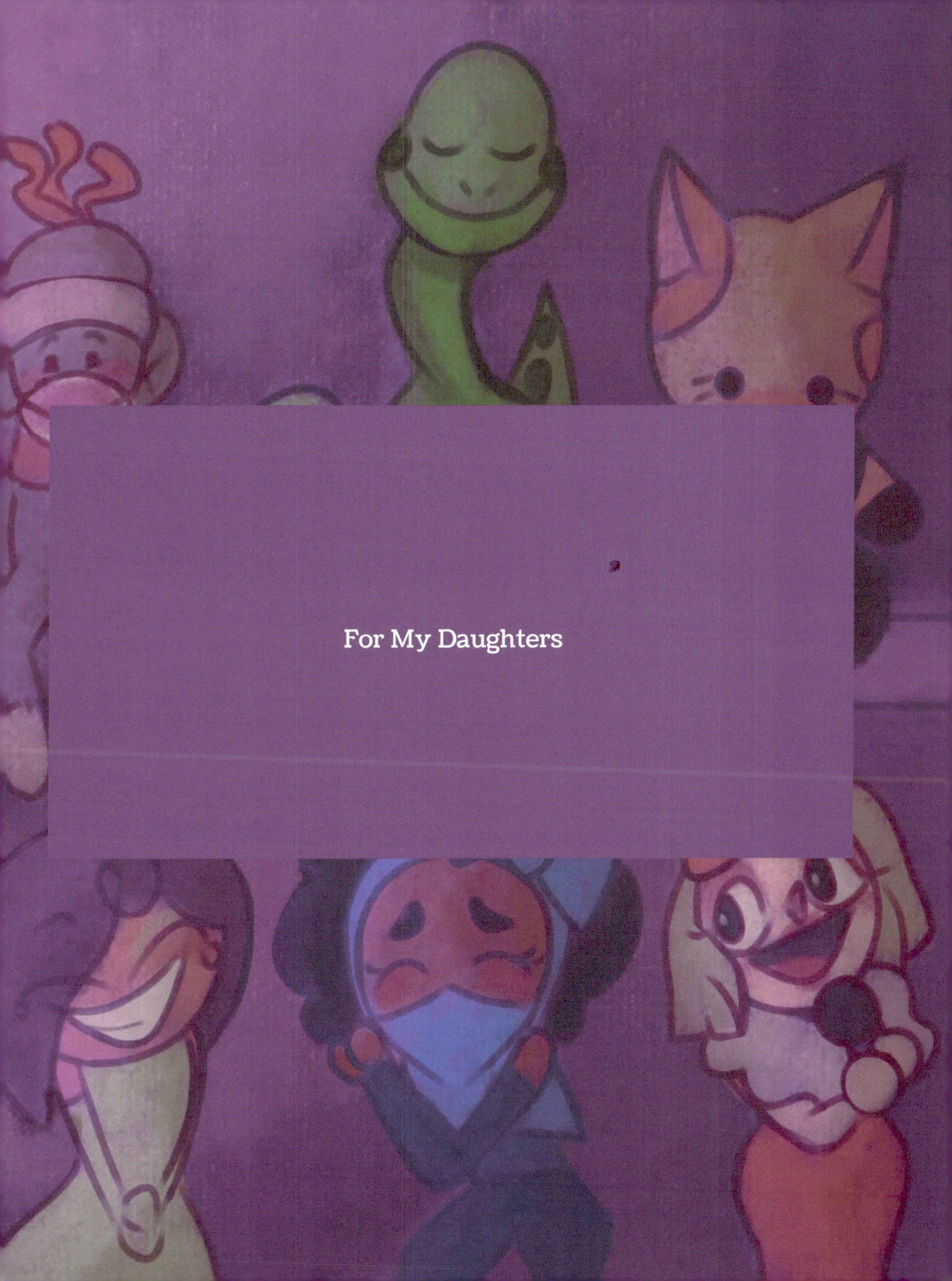

For My Daughters

Mr. Guffy's Toy Shoppe

Had all sorts of toys

Of all shapes and sizes

For all girls and boys.

One day the postman delivered

A very large crate.

But Mr. Guffy just left it

Because it was quite late.

He turned out the lights

And locked the shoppe door.

The toys were all waiting

For their time to explore.

The shoppe was now quiet.

The lights were all out.

The toys waited patiently

'Til they could all move about.

The clock on the wall
Just ticktocked away.
The toys couldn't wait
'Til it was time they could play.

Thirteen o'clock chimed,
The shoppes magical hour.
It was time for the toys
To use their secret toy-power.

The shoppe full of toys

Started moving around

Laughing and playing

Except the Toy Soldier

Who could only just frown.

The soldier had lots of friends,

He couldn't deny,

But there was no one just like him

And that made him cry.

"Wipe your tears, my brave soldier."
Was Dolly's sweet plea.
"We will help you be happy,
Come, you will see."

"Let's play some games,

Like What's In The Crate?"

Sock-monkey tried cheering

The sad soldier's fate.

Everyone wondered

What was inside.

New dollies? Some candy?

A bicycle to ride?

But the soldier didn't take part

In their guessing fun.

Whether it was poppets or puppies,

He was still a soldier of one.

The other toys tried

To fill him with cheer,

Because as a friend

He was really quite dear.

So the Circus Bears pranced

In their silly circus clothes,

And the Ballerinas danced

On their tip-tippy-toes,

While the Clowns juggled

And honked their red nose.

They wanted so badly

To turn his frown upright

So they laughed, danced, and sang,

All through the night.

Raggedy Annie had to know

What was in the crate,

Before Mr. Guffy could return

And it would be too late.

Raggedy Andy helped Annie
Pull on the crate tied with string.
The crate sprung open
Like a tightly wound spring!

Wooden Soldiers in straight-lines
Marched all around the room,
While Monkey crashed his cymbals
With a good marching tune.

The Lonely Toy Soldier

Was lonely no more!

He was happier now

Than ever before.

Everyone cheered the new

Wooden Soldier platoon,

While the planes in formation

Flew all around the room.

Everyone joined in until

The bright sun arose.

When they heard a key turn,

They all quickly froze.

Mr. Guffy was surprised

At the first thing he did see-

A toy shoppe full of happy toys

Like one big family!